YOUR SPECIAL
FRIEND

Your Special Friend

A Book for Peers of Children
Diagnosed with Asperger Syndrome

JOSIE SANTOMAURO

Illustrated by Carla Marino

Jessica Kingsley Publishers
London and Philadelphia

First published in 2009
by Jessica Kingsley Publishers
116 Pentonville Road
London N1 9JB, UK
and
400 Market Street, Suite 400
Philadelphia, PA 19106, USA

www.jkp.com

Library of Congress Cataloging in Publication Data
Santomauro, J. (Josie)
    Your special friend : a book for peers of children diagnosed with asperger syndrome /
Josie Santomauro ; Illustrated by Carla Marino.
        p. cm.
    ISBN 978-1-84310-661-6 (pb : alk. paper) 1. Asperger's syndrome--Popular works.
I. Marino, Carla. II. Title.
    RJ506.A9S367 2009
    618.92'858832--dc22

                                                    2008041439

British Library Cataloguing in Publication Data
A CIP catalogue record for this book is available from the British Library

ISBN 978 1 84310 661 6

Printed and bound in Great Britain by
Athenaeum Press, Gateshead, Tyne and Wear

Thank you to all the wonderful
contributors who have given
permission to reprint their gifts of
poetry, reflections, writings and
private thoughts here in this
book.

Contents

Friendship

Friendship is like a flower,
When it blooms it is beautiful.
Friendship is like a diamond,
Very precious and rare.
Friendship is like a hidden treasure,
You must search hard to find it.
Friendship is like a fire,
It keeps you warm inside.
Friendship is like a butterfly,
When found, is like redemption.
Friendship is honest,
Friendship is true,
Friendship is wonderful,
Friendship is you.
Friendship is like beautiful music
That echoes in our hearts,
Forever and ever and ever
…For eternity.

Welcome

Are you a friend, classmate or relative of a person with Asperger Syndrome? Then let's go on a journey to learn more about that person. If we understand them a little better, then we can all be a little more relaxed about how we behave around them, and they will feel better that you understand them a little more too.

- Do they get special help at school?

- Do they go to special classes to learn how to cope with teasing?

- Do they go to a special school to learn how to behave appropriately in class?

- Do they have a teaching assistant sit with them during class time?

- Why do you think they need all this extra help?

Let's find out why.

What's Wrong with My Friend?

Your friend needs extra help in four areas:

1. Social skills
2. Communication
3. Behaviour
4. Sensory stimulation.

When somebody needs help so they can function more easily in the community, they may have a disability.

Look at these different types of help others need:

- a person who needs a wheelchair to move around
- a person who needs glasses to see
- a person who needs a puffer for asthma
- a person who needs to use a cane to walk
- a person who needs help to speak clearer to be understood
- a person who needs a hearing aid to hear.

Asperger Syndrome?

When you add up these four areas:

1. needs help with social skills
2. needs help with talking and communicating with people
3. needs help with behaviour choices
4. needs help with sensory stimulation, as they can find bright lights or noise, for example, very stressful

they equal a disability called *Asperger Syndrome*.

Asperger Syndrome might make life seem a little hard for your friend

but

Asperger Syndrome also makes them very special.

And, because you are a caring and understanding friend…

You are special too!

Do you know anyone else who has a friend who has Asperger Syndrome?

Write the names of other special people like you here

. . . .

. . . .

. . . .

. . . .

Introducing
Asperger Syndrome

A nger and frustration

S tress and anxiety

P roblems with speech and language

E asily distracted

R eality/Fiction confusion

G ross motor skills

E ccentric or odd behaviours

R igid and doesn't like change

S ocial skills

Y our friend can be quite intelligent

N o eye contact

D oesn't like loud noises and crowds

R ote memory

O bsessional

M aking friends is hard

E mpathy

Let's Take a Closer Look at Asperger Syndrome

Anger and frustration

- Your friend may have temper tantrums when angry.
- They might find it hard to ask for help when feeling confused or frustrated.

Stress and anxiety

- They don't like to be teased.
- They can sometimes get anxious over changes.

- They can sometimes get stressed at school.
- They need help to learn how to relax and keep calm.
- They need help to ignore teasing and bullying.

Problems with speech and language

- Sometimes they don't realize that their voice is too loud.
- They may have an unusual voice.
- Sometimes they can't explain what they want to say.
- Sometimes they don't understand what people are telling them.

Easily distracted

- Maybe their room and school desk is always untidy.
- Sometimes they forget what someone said to them.
- Sometimes it's hard for them to pay attention, especially in a busy classroom.

Reality/Fiction confusion

- Sometimes they don't understand jokes or stories.

- They might believe that their dreams are real.

- They get confused if people say things like 'Pull your socks up'.

Gross motor skills

- Sometimes they can be clumsy.

- They might find some sports (especially ball games) a little hard to play.

Eccentric or odd behaviours

- They have different behaviours to other kids.
- Other kids might think they're a bit weird.
- They might do everyday things differently to everyone else.

Rigid and doesn't like change

- They like it better when things don't change.
- They really like things to stay the same.
- They like to know what is going to happen next.

Social skills

- They might find it hard to understand people's body language, like if someone's bored when they're talking.
- They like to talk about their hobbies all the time.
- They may not understand social 'rules' and can sometimes seem rude.

Your friend can be quite intelligent

- They may be very intelligent, especially at maths, science and computers.

- Some doctors call them 'little professor'.

- They may even go to university when they grow up.

No eye contact

- They don't like to look at people's eyes when they talk to them.

- They might look at the ground instead of someone's face, but they are still listening to them.

Doesn't like loud noises and crowds

- Loud noises can hurt their ears, and bright light may hurt their eyes.

- They don't like noisy or crowded places, like shopping centres or parties.

Rote memory

- They might remember things that happened a long time ago.

- They have a good memory for facts and figures.

Obsessional

- If they really like one or two things they can talk on and on…and on…about it.

- They can do or say something over and over, like flapping their hands, touching their face or repeating a word.

Making friends is hard

- They might not have a lot of friends.

- They might like to have more friends.

- They might not be interested in friends.

- They sometimes find it hard to make new friends.

Empathy

- Sometimes they can't understand how other people are feeling – like if someone is happy or sad.

But here are some other features of Asperger Syndrome:

A rtistic	**S** ignificant
S mart	**Y** why? Asks lots of questions
P unctual	**N** atural
E ngaging	**D** etermined
R epetitive movements	**R** esourceful
G ood natured	**O** ver sensitive
E xtraordinary	**M** aths wiz
R ules	**E** motional

Why Has Your Friend Got Asperger Syndrome?

How did they get Asperger Syndrome?

- They didn't catch it like when you catch a cold or the chicken pox.

- It's not their fault or their parents' – it's nobody's fault!

- They were probably born like that – but nobody knew until they grew up a bit.

- There is no special cure or magic potion to fix Asperger Syndrome.

- Doctors think a small part of their brain is working differently to other people's.

They're not the only one!

At least one in every 150 people in the world has Asperger Syndrome.

How to Learn More about Asperger Syndrome

Join the local Asperger Syndrome support group.

Chat on the internet with other people who know people with Asperger Syndrome.

Talk to your parents or school counsellor.

Read books about Asperger Syndrome.

Talk to your friend/relative/classmate who has Asperger Syndrome.

The AS Princess

Written and illustrated by a girl in 1999 when she was about ten years old, she expresses how she is feeling at the time about having Asperger Syndrome.

Once upon a time there was a princess. She was born with a disability, which was called Asperger Syndrome. Her name was Alexia. Alex for short. She went to a co-ed school for princes and princesses. Now she was often very naughty. Once she went off in the middle of a game at the park, and went off to pick flowers. The principal came after her. She hated maths so she would run off in the maths lesson. One day she went to a special school. Here she learned to be better, but everyone at her primary school called it a mental clinic. She was very upset. Everyone teased her about it. But she doesn't mind it much now.

The End

How Can You Help Your Friend?

By learning to help them you are:

- helping them to have a happy life

and

- helping them to be a successful citizen.

Time out

- If you notice your friend becoming really stressed at home or at school, you can remind them to take themselves to time out.

Diary

- Remind them to look at their school diary every day.

- Remind them to write in the dates of any changes or new things that are going to happen, like birthdays or lessons.

Change

- Warn your friend about changes they don't know about.

- Remind them about where you are going or what is about to happen.

- Even draw a picture for them, or write down what you know.

Positive

- When they are feeling sad, think of things they like to do and play their favourite game with them.

- Laugh and have fun with them.

Charts

- Remind them to look at their charts and timetables.

- You can even help them make their charts.

- Perhaps you might even like to make some charts of your own!

What about You?

Just because you have a friend/relative/classmate with a disability, that doesn't mean you're not special.

Here are some suggestions for you:

Talk

- Talk to your mum, dad or your carer, or even your grandma; somebody special who listens to you when you feel a little sad or even angry.

Journal

- Keep a journal or a diary at home for yourself.
- Write in it your thoughts and feelings.
- Try to write in it every day.

Positive

- When you're feeling sad, do something that makes you feel good, like playing with your pet or reading a story.

- Laugh and have fun.

Dial-a-smile

- Collect pictures from magazines, cartoons, photos and drawings that you like and paste them into a scrapbook.

- Feel like relaxing? Or need to be cheered up? Have a look at your Dial-a-smile book!

Mixed Feelings

Sometimes you might feel like you hate your friend/ relative/ classmate.

They annoy you, and sometimes they're treated differently to you. You might feel like it's just not fair! Sometimes they might even be embarrassing!

It's ok for you to have feelings like this. Remember it's their behaviour that you don't like, not the person.

Label the left side of the weighing scales 'Dislikes' and the other 'Likes'.

On the 'Dislikes' side write the things you find annoying about your friend.

Most of the time you will like your friend. They might be funny and smart. Write on the 'Likes' side of the scales all the things you like about them.

Discover what happens to the scales...

Always remember:
The Likes will always outweigh the Dislikes!

Write an Acrostic Using Your Name

An acrostic is a series of words where the first letters of each line spell out another word or phrase.

Use special words about you.

For example, if your name is Sam:

    S uper

    A rtistic

    M usician

Remember everybody has a disability of some kind,
It might be big or small.
They might need lots of help
Or none at all.
A disability might be if someone can't swim, can't read,
Needs help with maths or even if they have a big mole
On their nose!
You might even have a disability of some kind.
We're all individuals in this world.
Nobody is perfect!
(Not even the Prime Minister or the President!)
Shhh!! Don't tell them I said that!

Visit Josie's website: www.booksbyjosie.com.au